SOCIAL FORCES
IN SOUTHEAST ASIA

PUBLISHED ON THE EDWARD F. WAITE FUND

This book contains three lectures delivered at Smith College in April 1947, and constitutes the second of a series of volumes of Smith College lectures.

Social Forces
IN SOUTHEAST ASIA

by

CORA DU BOIS

UNIVERSITY OF MINNESOTA PRESS

LONDON · GEOFFREY CUMBERLEGE · OXFORD UNIVERSITY PRESS

PRINTED IN THE UNITED STATES OF AMERICA
BY THE NORTH CENTRAL PUBLISHING COMPANY
ST. PAUL, MINNESOTA

PREFACE

"NOTHING can distort the true picture of conditions and events in this world more than to regard one's own country as the center of the universe, and to view all things solely in their relationship to this fixed point. It is inevitable that such a method of observation should create an entirely false perspective. Yet this is the only method admitted and used by the seventy or eighty national governments of our world, by our legislators and diplomats, by our press and radio. . . .

"Within such a contorted system of assumed fixed points, it is easy to demonstrate that the view taken from each point corresponds to reality. If we admit and apply this method, the viewpoint of every single nation appears indisputably correct and wholly justified. But we arrive at a hopelessly confused and grotesque over-all picture of the world."

EMERY REVES, *The Anatomy of Peace*

IN ORDER that the reader should not be misled, it must be stated at the outset that these lectures are not a scientific treatise on Southeast Asia by an anthropologist, although my professional training is in anthropology and my interest is in southern Asia. Rather, the purpose of these lectures is to give interpretive insights such as essayists often advance. Neither the theory of cultural anthropology nor the intimate knowledge of Southeast Asia is sufficiently developed to permit greater precision on so broad but so legitimate a canvass.

I presume that no one gives a series of lectures and commits them to print without assigning value to the undertaking. The value inherent in this undertaking rests on a deep conviction, shared by others who know the area through direct experience, that forces are at work in Southeast Asia which deserve the most judicious attention of diplomats, the best analysis by social scientists, and a highly serious interest on the part of all responsible people in the Western world.

CONTENTS

7

Chapter I

SOME GENERAL CONCEPTS

THE generalizations and speculations which constitute the major part of this book cannot be considered scientific in any serious or rigorous definition of the word. They are frankly the distillates offered by a writer who was trained in the social sciences and who has been engrossed in an area. The objectives, however, do approximate the goals that social scientists working on an area may well set themselves. The faith of science is that the universe is ordered and that such order can be detected by human intelligence. Therefore, social sciences are concerned with discovering what is consistent and regular in human behavior. When their observations are accurate, social scientists will be able to predict the continuance of these regularities into future events over shorter or longer time spans.

Cultural anthropology is such a social science. It is concerned with man as a social and psychological phenomenon, and attempts to analyze the forces operative on him in his total environment. Regional studies are concerned with all aspects, human and natural, of an area defined geographically. There is obviously no conflict between the two and yet very few attempts have been made to bring theoretic anthropology to bear on the practical problems of a region. Dr. Benedict's recent book on Japan, *The Chrysanthemum and the Sword*, is one of the few notable exceptions.

The reason for a failure to be practical may lie in the fact that anthropology still possesses no serious and generally acceptable theoretical structure. Cultural studies are still in need of their Einstein, their Darwin, or their Mendel. Neither Marx nor Freud are adequate, stimulating as they have proved to our thinking about Western European culture. They have failed by overgeneralizing not only a single aspect of man's social existence but also by overgeneralizing on the basis of a Western European variety of man in a particular period.

As to regionalists, they existed long before 1941, but the war greatly accentuated interest in this approach. Anthropologists have long stressed the interrelation of all phenomena which affect man in his environment. They have also known that part of that environment is self-generated; that it is social; that it springs from man's deeply gregarious impulses. During the war, however, no such academic formulations influenced minds concerned with military problems. The stark and inescapable necessities of the military situation forced consideration of social data, as well as of geographic and biologic phenomena. They were facts with which to deal. Social theories went by the board largely because they were not adequately illuminating to practical action.

The relation between man as a biologic and psychologic unit on the one hand, and as a product of his geographic and social environment on the other hand, has been widely perceived both theoretically and practically but without a structured theory adequate to guide practice.

However, during the war many different kinds of scientific specialists were assembled to apply their knowledge and techniques to regions of military interest. Although this collaborative experience has no abstract formulation, the war has greatly accelerated inter-disciplinary thinking; the walls separating the social sciences as practiced in universities and as practical fields of social action are crumbling with increasing rapidity. People are learning to think, as well as feel, about the kind of world in which they wish to live. If they do not, there is little hope for the continued existence of any world we know.

I venture to predict that increasingly education will be phrased in terms of problems and theories rather than in terms of areas or disciplines like Southeast Asia and anthropology.

It is to this task, however falteringly and hesitantly, that I have committed myself. There exist a few conceptual tools for understanding the world in which we live. They are neither complete nor sharp. But such as they are they may be worth reviewing.

In discussing concepts that assist in understanding the forces at work in society today, let us begin first with that of culture itself. By culture social scientists usually mean the relationships between human beings; between human beings and their environment, both social and physical; and between the institutions human beings create to implement such relationships. People without culture are inconceivable. Similarly culture without man is meaningless. Both are constantly interactive. Anthropology recognizes the validity of such partial interpretations as biologic man, psychological man, economic man; and the political animal, the religious animal, the ethical animal. But it insists that all of these insights, and many more, are the essence of a broader generalization which it calls culture.

Society is the more limited term generally used for the

forms and institutions employed by human beings to structure their gregarious existence. Society, then, is a part of culture. Nothing can be more tedious than quarrels about definitions. We could pause here and cite dozens of authorities who have given varying interpretations to the words culture and society. For our purposes *society* will be used here to mean the formal patterns of gregarious life whereas *culture* includes not only society but all the value systems and the emotional repercussions on people of living together in whatever phase of history or part of the world.

It is the interacting whole and the processes that shape and direct this whole which concern the anthropologist. As you perceive, he is not modest in his goals. This in turn may explain why he has not yet been more successful in formulating a satisfactory basic theory of culture. Nevertheless, this idea of culture as synthesis is important. It is important because it is dynamic. It demands insights into relationships. It goes beyond descriptive categories. The word culture will seem rich or empty to the extent that one has learned to think of orders of relationships rather than of items, to the extent that one has acquired a view of the world that transcends immediate location in time and space, and to the extent that one has brought to the level of consciousness the arbitrary quality of what one calls "perfectly natural," "common sense," "right and wrong."

Culture, like the individual psyche, or like an iceberg, is only fractionally a part of one's conscious equipment. The last thing of which the deep sea fish would be aware is the ocean. In respect to culture, most human beings resemble all too closely the fish at the bottom of the sea. Large parts of culturally determined behavior are so imbedded in our characters that they are "perfectly natural." How you point, when or how you laugh and cry, what you consider edible, the proprieties of sex and procreation — these are things everyone learns as surely as he learns table manners and how to spell. The task of every person today who feels a serious sense of citizenship is to expand his cultural horizons by evaluating his own cultural heritage, at the same time that he fathoms and makes useful increasing portions of his total mind, as opposed to his logical and conscious one. The history of our generation dare not be written by the near-sighted. Our responsibilities are too great and too urgent.

This brings us to a second concept deeply engrained in anthropological thinking: culture is relative. By that anthropologists really mean that cultural values are relative. If one examines what has seemed good and true, or bad and false, in different societies of the world over a stretch of both time and space, one comes to realize that different peoples have preferred to stress for approval (and equally important, for disapproval) only a segment of the various virtues and vices known to man. Although certain forces appear to be constant and certain patterns are generalized, no absolute values are yet apparent from a study of man's gregarious life as he has fashioned it in many places during many millenia. This does not mean that they do not exist, nor that they should not be sought for. It simply means that for the time being we have observed peoples who consider peace rather than war a virtue; that there are peoples to whom leisure rather than labor is the ultimate good. There are still other peoples who have preferred to stress ecstatic emotional states rather than reason. In some social groups a free and undisciplined child is considered more charming than a precocious and well-mannered one. In some societies, the admirable person is not one who departs from the accepted

13

norm but rather one who most thoroughly conforms to it and who most brilliantly executes the traditional pattern of life. To Americans this is a particularly difficult and incomprehensible value. There are even some cultures which have survived long, happily, and productively without placing the somewhat obsessional value we do on bathtubs, plumbing, and personal hygiene. There are cultures whose cynosure is not the eternally youthful and beautiful woman of advertising copy and Hollywood.

In the midst of such observations the social scientist, as scientist, is still too confused and fallible as a person to formulate an ultimate ethic. He is still too much the prisoner of his own culture to do more than observe and describe, somewhat wryly, the scene he sees. Like so many other types of scientists he is at this point ready to surrender his problems to the ethical philosopher with whose brashness he will immediately quarrel.

So far we have considered two concepts: that of culture itself and the idea that cultural values are relative, with the implication that scientists *qua* scientists are by no means ready to deal with ethics objectively. A third basic concept of most social scientists is that culture is dynamic. Culture is constantly changing. At no time and in no place has it been observed at rest. It is true that social scientists speak of stable cultures, but this means only that the rate of change at any given time seems slower in some societies than in others.

Also, within any one culture, one can observe periods of acceleration and periods of relative, but only relative, quiescence. At times the gradients of change are steep; at other times they level off. The rate of change in European culture, for example, has been highly accelerated in the last five hundred years. In the last few centuries Europeans have even

14

made a virtue of social changes and have called that virtue *progress.* Japan, on the other hand, was quiescent during the Tokugawa period. We all know too intimately the acceleration which it underwent after the Meiji restoration and which it still seems to be experiencing.

In cultural changes two major interacting forces can be detected: the centrifugal, and the centripetal. The centrifugal or expansive vigor of culture is often called diffusion.

Strictly speaking, cultural diffusion occurs only when that totality which we call culture overlays and engrosses a geographic area. For example, the occupation of the North American continent by peoples of European stock was a case of total cultural diffusion. North of the Rio Grande in less than three hundred and fifty years Indian cultures to all intents and purposes essentially disappeared. This does not mean that a considerable number of Indians have not survived but that their cultural integrity has almost entirely vanished. In its place there exists in the same area a variant of the kind of life conceived in Europe of the Reformation and transplanted by immigrating Europeans.

This instance of cultural vigor is not unique. Judging only from archeological remains, Neolithic culture may have had the same expansive energy. The early city-states of the Tigris-Euphrates Valley had comparable centrifugal energy. The Islamic peoples were distinguished for the speed and vigor of their cultural expansion. The potentialities of modern Russian society in this direction are a source of grave concern in the contemporary world. Why, how, and when total cultures go on all-out, expansionistic rampages during which they feel the need to eliminate the opposition they meet in other cultures is one of the vital problems facing social scientists today.

15

But in addition to this totalistic type of expansion, there are lesser manifestations to be observed: the diffusion of the component parts of a culture in the form of culture traits, culture complexes, or consciously held culture values. These partial expansions operate selectively both in terms of the giver and the receiver. For example, in the sixteenth century the Portuguese were, consciously at least, concerned with spreading Christianity. In the eighteenth century the Dutch were in search of trade. In the nineteenth century the British were concerned with the white man's burden. I do not believe that such conscious value systems can, or should, be discounted. The conscious motives were partly effective whatever other factors they masked. However, reverting to the earlier figure of speech about icebergs, I am firmly convinced that overt motives seldom suffice to explain cultural dynamics adequately. They smack too much of that well-known psychological mechanism known as rationalization.

Let us now examine some partial, less value-ladened instances of diffusion, where traits spread with no attempt at conscious rationalization on the part of the giver. Classical examples of the latter are the way Indian corn was accepted as a staple crop throughout large areas of the world after the European discovery of the New World; the way the use of tobacco appealed to varied cultures once it was exported from the Western Hemisphere; or the immediate and widespread delight in European matches. The speed with which these traits spread and were accepted far exceeded the expansive vigor of even Europe's age of discovery and its commercial revolution. Perhaps we have here a basic cultural generalization. Namely that culture traits spread more rapidly than total cultures or even than culturally held values and, as a further refinement, that technology and material efficiencies take hold more easily than value systems. Perhaps this tentative generalization may be explained by the assumption that material efficiencies are less deeply rooted in the emotional nexus of individuals than are value systems.

Cultural change viewed from the centripetal or integrative point of view appears to present a different series of forces. In this area of change, the first process which strikes the eye is the absorptive one and simultaneously the high degree of selectivity and of reinterpretation which occurs when foreign traits or complexes impinge upon a social group. For example, Islamic culture was deeply reinterpreted in Persia. The Buddhism of China or Japan is not only profoundly different from Buddhism in Ceylon or Burma; it has also been put to different social uses. Or in a more trivial vein, tea when first introduced in Europe was considered primarily a medicine; the parasol, which is the symbol of rank in Southeast Asia, became a sunshade or umbrella in Europe. In some cases the resistance to absorption is noteworthy. Christianity as a religious system has made little headway against Islam or Buddhism. Patriotism in the nationalistic sense has had but the most limited success against the familistic system of China. Marxian thought has had little appeal in the successful system of free capitalistic enterprise in the United States.

The point to be made is that the receiving culture either resists, selects, or reinterprets what impinges upon it from the outside. When absorptions of new traits occur over a wide field of cultural activities whole new cultural constellations may be created. This situation I believe to be the case in large parts of Asia today. It has certainly been true of Japan in the last seventy years.

When resistance has been strong, vigorous diffusional

forces have been stayed. Thus the Christian world at least twice resisted the persuasive as well as the military aspects of Islam — once in the eighth and once in the seventeenth centuries. When material forces are at least somewhat in balance, the degree of absorption and reinterpretation of new cultural material is probably directly related to the degree of pre-existing integration in the receiving culture.

This brings us to the subject of cultural integration. A culture is conceived by anthropologists as a series of institutions, patterns of individual and interpersonal behavior, and systems of beliefs, all delicately interlinked. Culture is not simply a group of independent traits that only need to be added together in order to be understood. Culture is not a sum of parts; it is rather a series of more or less efficiently intermeshed gears. To the outsider the linkages frequently seem arbitrary or obscure. To the insider this linkage is taken so much for granted, is so deeply part of a system of subconscious beliefs, that it is rarely perceived and even more rarely challenged. That is why it is often easier to grasp the integrative sequences in a foreign culture than in one's own. That is why American anthropologists, despite constant challenges, have failed to write a convincing account of American culture; and even were a foreigner to write such an account, it might meet with wide disbelief among Americans.

As an example of integration let us examine the so-called institution of marriage in our culture. Before discussing this particular case two points should be interpolated: first every known society has some form of marriage — in other words, it is a universal institution; second, when marriage as it is found in many different societies is compared, the only common denominator that remains appears to be the device of associating men and women in order to localize children in their society.

It is obvious that marriage among ourselves has associated with it many more functions and values than this universal one. In our culture, it not only performs the universal function of placing the child in a social context, but in addition it sets the approved limits of sexual gratification and procreation. In many cultures sexual activity and procreation are not limited by marital arrangements. Marriage in our culture is also linked with that greatly ramified institution — the law. This in turn links marriage to the state and to all the values invested in legality. Usually religious approval is required for marriage in our society. And religion with us is not only a set of supernatural beliefs; it is also a system of ethics and a vastly wealthy and elaborately structured institution. In addition, marriage in our society sets the customary middle-class economic roles of men and women. It defines man's economic responsibilities in terms of the producer and breadwinner; to women it assigns managerial and household responsibilities. These roles again are given legal support in the shape of such customs as alimony, inheritance, and joint property. Marriage determines the names that women and children will bear and the kind of residence approved for the biologic unit. It influences our kinship nomenclature and interfamily relations. In other words it is linked with a whole series of institutions, values, and personal relationships which we take so much for granted that its peculiar, arbitrary, and integrated quality rarely occurs to us.

I do not wish to dwell unduly on a single example of integration. It is used only to indicate the fashion in which our own culture has woven together a wide range of institutional, psychological, and ethical materials at its disposal. The example of marriage in our culture is used to stress the point that these complexes are often not perceived as arbitrary until one has learned to view human behavior and social phenomena comparatively.

The next point that should be made concerning the integrative processes of culture is that when a change occurs in any one link of the series, reverberations are felt throughout the structure of society. For example, when the power of the church over the lay world began to recede, the way was opened for marriages to cease being a religious concern. On the other hand when the state expanded and its power permeated an increasingly larger sphere of the individual's activities, the importance of marriage as a legal concern was stressed. As the patriarchal system of Europe disintegrated and the economic dependence of women altered, the system of dowries waned while ideas of joint property emerged.

With such concepts and cases in mind practical investigations suggest themselves. For example, if the previously cited complex which constitutes marriage in the United States is considered in the light of the present housing shortage, what are the repercussions on residence patterns? Will alterations in this one area of an interlinked system affect divorce laws, alimony, the socialization of children, and so forth? Further one wonders what specifically may happen when this set of reverberations interlocks with factors which are changing at a faster or slower rate? Where will gears be stripped and where will they interlock more smoothly as the result of changes in tempo?

Change, then, can and does appear in different areas of culture and, like a set of interlocking gear systems, it sets in motion a whole series of other changes from which new patterns of relationship emerge. In some cases a particular aspect of society changes more slowly than the others. In such a case we speak of cultural lags. The case of technology in the United States as compared to legislative procedures or international relations is a well known and deeply serious example of the way in which one phase of culture may change more rapidly than another with all of its attendant dislocations. Policy formulations and legislation rarely do more than institutionalize widely accepted ideas and practices. Furthermore, in a culture whose acceleration is high, lags may well be numerous and more obvious than in slow-moving cultures.

When a social custom has entirely lost its original function it is called a survival. The classical examples are the persistence of Latin and Hebrew in liturgy. In some cases such survivals are given secondary reinterpretations. The banner used to lead men into battle is now the flag of a nation whose professed goal is peace. These reinterpretations, these transfers of pattern, are important in Southeast Asia although they are not unique to the area. But whether we are confronted with a lag or a survival, we may be sure to find them used symbolically for strong emotional investment by certain sections of the social group. They are, therefore, not inert phenomena but genuine forces in the social scheme.

It is implicit in what has been said about cultural change that the degree of integration to be observed at any period in time may vary between cultures. At a given period some peoples have so skillfully interwoven the many aspects of gregarious existence into a single and apparently coherent pattern that we speak of their social life as highly integrat-

21

ed. This does not mean that there are no odds and ends of custom and belief left floating about, but that the bulk of the behavior and beliefs of people in a highly integrated society seem consistent and beyond question in terms of their own premises. One finds societies of this type frequently in small primitive communities. But China, at least during certain periods of its past, appeared highly integrated. Certainly nineteenth century England gave a similar impression.

It should be stressed that a high degree of integration does not mean that all people have the same achievement goals. A society which offers two, or even many, goals may also be (although not necessarily) a single well-integrated whole. For a century prior to the Civil War, the South had quite different life patterns and goals for the plantation owner and the Negro slave. Their two roles were clearly defined and the relationships well adjusted to form a single entity. This cultural solution might have persisted far longer had not the growth of economic and moral forces in the world impinged upon it. The caste system of Hindu India was another case of a society which offered many and varied goals but which was nevertheless a highly integrated culture that persisted successfully for centuries.

In a multiple-goal, integrated society, the class or caste structure frequently serves as one of the most rewarding social institutions for study. The economic roles played by such classes form a highly significant part of the picture.

The integration of a society begins to crack, not because goals differ in the society, but because they lose their compelling quality as the result of changes (1) in value systems, (2) in interpersonal relations, (3) in the class structure, and (4) in the economy. Contrary to the dogma of economic determinism which underlies so much of the

Western European social research of the last century, I believe that marked alterations in any one aspect of culture can set off a sequence of profound changes in the culture as a whole. The invention of printing, the personality of Gandhi, or the influence of Freudian psychology are cases in point.

Another point should be made in relation to the goals a society sets. There is scarcely a social group whose practice does not depart to some extent from its overtly expressed or its covert goals. In surveying the societies of the world with which any nation has to deal in its international relations, nothing could be more misleading than to accept uncritically what they say and believe their theories and values to be without checking them against actual practice. For example, the Russian theory of the dictatorship of the proletariat has little relation to the practice of party dictatorship now exercised in the USSR.

There is another and more specialized aspect to be considered in relation to the goals set by a society. When goals are competitive very few persons in the culture are able to achieve them. There is little room at the top of a pyramid. Unless fairly satisfactory alternate goals are possible, the majority of the people in a competitive society do not find life a steady and progressive gratification, nor is their attitude toward their peers as they climb upward likely to be generous. If the small American boy cannot be president of the United States he should at least be able to settle for a bank presidency. Otherwise he may seek to scale the pyramid by becoming public enemy No. I.

This situation — a low degree of integration, with wide gaps between theory and practice, and a competitive society — is one thoroughly familiar to us here in the United

States for certainly a century. It is a situation that exists to-day in far more turbulent forms in many other parts of the world, and particularly in many of the so-called less developed areas of the world. To greater or lesser degrees all parts of the non-European world have been disequilibrated, or if you wish, disintegrated by the impact of an expanding European culture. The problems presented by such disintegrations are far too little understood by social scientists and statesmen. On the whole we are far too uninformed and too indifferent to such problems for the intelligent execution of our own nation's grave responsibilities in international affairs.

Since actual research testing the type of assumptions and the concepts just discussed cannot be completed rapidly for all areas of the world, and since certain areas of the world are not open to research teams of social scientists, a second best is an attempt to speculate with such conceptual tools and such data as we now possess. That the results cannot be definitive is obvious. Yet so urgent have the practical problems of certain parts of the world become that even dull tools are better than none. Such is the situation in Southeast Asia and such is the attempt in the next two chapters.

Chapter II

SOME SOCIAL FACTORS DISCERNIBLE IN THE SOUTHEAST ASIA OF 1940

SOUTHERN Asia stretches from the subcontinent of India to the Australian subcontinent. Within it Southeast Asia is encompassed. From Karachi in Pakistan to Melbourne in Australia is some 6600 miles. From Melbourne to northern Luzon in the Philippines is some 4100 air miles. From northern Luzon back to Karachi is approximately another 3500 miles.

In the center of this great south Asian triangle lie the variously specialized cultures of Southeast Asia: on the Indochinese Peninsula are Burma, Siam, Indochina, and Malaya; on the island arc at its base, the archipelagoes of Indonesia and the Philippines.

In the large south Asian triangle live almost six hundred million people or approximately 25 percent of humanity—a humanity so cheaply counted in European minds (if not in their own) that millions of them have died of starvation in the last five years with scarcely a headline in our newspapers as obituary. India with its four hundred million is the center of population gravity for the area. But Indonesia has seventy million of whom fifty million are concentrated in Java alone. Burma has seventeen million and Siam about eighteen million; Indochina's population is about

twenty-five million; the Philippines now is considered to have seventeen million. And Malaya, the former hub of European military strategy in this region, counts in all a mere six million. The ten or more millions of Australia and New Zealand, as well as the uncounted hundreds of thousands of people on scattered and seldom mentioned islands, are inevitably within the orbit of south Asian affairs.

Immediately to the north of this great south Asian center of potentially important humanity lies another population center: China with its four hundred million. And China cannot be ignored even when one concentrates on southern Asia. Regions and areas, like fields of academic learning, are artificial boundaries which we erect around our curiosity. They do not represent limits of integrated reality, but defenses built to encompass the frailties of human comprehension.

Although the forces working in southern Asia are intimately bound up with the internal affairs of India, Australia, and China, discussion will concentrate chiefly on Southeast Asia. In this south Asian region as a whole and its interior area of Southeast Asia a new world is shaping itself out of its own indigenous traditions stimulated by the expansive energies of Hindu, Islamic, Chinese, and European cultures. There is probably no other area of the world so richly endowed with diverse cultural strains and so prepared to view the world tolerantly. Even if this area were not so richly endowed with varied cultural traditions, so large, so populous, so wealthy in human and material resources, it might still be culturally vital. Greece was such a case. But size, number, and wealth are meaningful values to the Western, and particularly the American, mind.

First let us glance briefly at some of the types of cultures

27

that have diffused into Southeast Asia, not in detailed historic fashion but only to identify some of the major cultural strands that have contributed to the present pattern. For almost two thousand years Southeast Asia has been a low pressure area on which more vigorous and expansive cultures have impinged. During the first centuries of the Christian era it was an area of low population, of tribally organized, animistic peoples whose cultural sophistication was derived from an intrusive fringe of Hindu and Buddhist settlements. That Indianization is still detectable, is still deeply rooted in many of the basic values of the area.

Into southern Asia next moved Islam. It made serious inroads on northern India, leaving behind its present troublesome political aftermath of Pakistan and India. To the south, Islam, as it diffused, flowed around the Buddhist countries like Ceylon, Burma, Siam, and parts of Indochina. But it engulfed Malaya and the larger part of Indonesia. Islam spent itself in the southern islands of the Philippines where today the Mohammedan Moros and the Christianized Tagalogs face each other within the framework of a new statehood.

Meanwhile a less dramatic, a less familiar, but nevertheless important and persistent stream of Mongoloid peoples, bearing the frontier culture of China, were pushing southward down into the Indochinese peninsula. The Hinduistic city-states gradually crumbled before their steady and little-known expansion. The nominal suzerainty of China was established over large parts of the area. Sinitic languages, like Thai and Annamese, are spoken today in the area by some forty-two million people. And China's long political memory still dwells from time to time on the rich areas along its southern borders. You will recall that it was a Chinese army which moved south to the sixteenth parallel in Indochina after V-J day. Recently available translations of Chiang Kai-shek's book, *China's Destiny*, remind one that imperial aspirations have not been forgotten.

In the sixteenth century, European culture first touched the edges of this melting pot. It remained largely peripheral, scarcely noticed by the peoples who were working out their own historically complex destinies. The dynastic wars and intrigues of the courts and the simple community life of artisan and farmer were left largely undisturbed for two centuries after the arrival of the Portuguese. However significant the development of direct contact with the Orient may have seemed to the European trader, in southern Asia he appeared as little more than a gnat on their horizons.

But as Europe passed from the commercial to the industrial revolution, as the centrifugal force of European culture gathered strength, the scene in southern Asia also changed. Colonialism replaced commercialism. Direct administration, raw materials, and markets for consumers' goods — in sum the idea of empire — grew in the Occident and encroached upon the Orient. The details of that period from roughly 1750 to 1940 have been widely studied by European historians, but characteristically from the viewpoint primarily of Europe.

In connection with these highlights on the cultural diffusions which affected Southeast Asia, it must be remembered that rates of change vary between cultures and within cultures; that there are varying tempos between the component parts of a culture which produce cultural lags and survivals; and that cultural absorption is selective.

In respect to Hinduistic influences, Buddhism, which has all but disappeared in India today, still thrives vigorously in Ceylon, Burma, and Siam. In a sense these Buddhist countries form a survivalistic block in respect to India and the religious changes which have occurred there. But since Buddhism and Hinduism have common roots, in comparison to other areas and religious complexes, there are detectable similarities.

Mohammedanism, which dominates the island world of much of Southeast Asia, has become, by reinterpretation and dilution, a far less fanatic and intense religion than it is in its Arabic hearthland. The Pan-Islamic movement has never gripped the imagination of the Mohammedans of Southeast Asia. As a result they have been able to root themselves more deeply in their own cultural life.

Both of these religions, with many of their embedded values, have not only escaped the types of changes which occurred in their hearthland, they have also proved firm bulwarks against Christianity and therefore have shut out one of the important media of Europeanization. In abstract language we say that these two institutions have been integrated to the local culture, have been relatively stable thereafter, and have formed barriers to other diffusionistic forces.

From the point of view of historical impacts one more point should be made concerning cultural changes in the area. Europe, in its four centuries of contact with Southeast Asia, has changed infinitely more rapidly than the Southeast Asian countries. This means that the cultural pressures from Europe have not always been coherent and consistent. Theoretically it is conceivable that this may have retarded the total influence of European culture on the area.

In any event Southeast Asia viewed from the outside has represented a singularly stable, almost survivalistic phenomenon — a low pressure area in the rising tide of world Europeanization. As ethnocentric Europeans we are therefore inclined to characterize these cultures as backward.

We have so far been examining the external impacts on Southeast Asian culture. Let us now face the other way and try to determine what new forces had really developed in Southeast Asia during the period of European colonialism and were in ferment there at the time of the Japanese invasion during the winter of 1941-42.

In diagnosing cultural changes, obviously all phenomena from climate through personality should be carefully weighed. This will not be possible in this brief a compass and, more importantly, because there is a distressing lack of information on the area.

We shall have to base our diagnoses on only a few social structures about which a little is known and on a few attitudes unscientifically estimated. I shall not use the term feudalism in discussing Southeast Asian society. There is to my mind a vast difference between the European lord and his land-bound serfs on the one hand and the magico-religious god-king symbolizing a world order in Southeast Asia. In Southeast Asia, but certainly not in Europe, the wealth and the sexual potency of the ruler, the splendor of the court and the temples were projected and sublimated expressions of cultural well-being. The lords seem to have been less the masters of serfs and more an expression of the peasantry's greatness. The state was not the exclusive, aggressive structure of European nationalism but was rather the symbol of a world order, and the expression of a system of proprieties in human and superhuman relationships.

Instead of drawing unprofitable analogies, it may be more useful to examine the pattern of the class structure and economy, the new philosophic ideas and values as they existed in Southeast Asia in 1940 — that is, after their relatively slow-moving cultures had been prodded for several centuries by Europe.

31

The class structure is often one of the most significant diagnostic phenomena we can use in the study of a society. But again, as in the case of feudalism, it will be necessary to voice a few warnings against the context of the word state, which we are forced to use for lack of a better one. *State* must be understood as a world order of a magico-religious variety and not a power system of the military-economic variety developed in Europe. It was the symbol of a religiously conceived order of social and supernatural relationships. Again, by way of warning, *class* as it will be used does not imply class struggle. It is used solely to describe hierarchical structure. There was no conflict between classes in the old cultures of Southeast Asia. Rather, the contrary situation appears to have existed: the complete mutual acceptance of respective roles. Remember that Marxian philosophy and the obsessional European preoccupation with a pair of opposites which are by definition irreconcilable had not yet entered the scene. Even today this European preoccupation with conflicting polarities has not succeeded in completely altering the sense of complementary mutuality in the exercise of social functions.

In Southeast Asia there existed at the time of European contact a two-class system. There was, and is, the vast rural peasantry living on as much land as it could well cultivate with its simple technology and depending primarily on irrigated rice as its staple food. Life centered in small compact villages. It entailed an immediately comprehensible, human, and rewarding series of duties and interpersonal obligations. The orientation of the peasant was communal and traditional. The goal of life was to raise rice and a family within a social purview which embraced, and still embraces, seldom more than a few hundred people. Gods were local and frequently animistic. The priests and diviners were also neighborhood men of little more learning than the peasant himself, but they were respected symbols of the orderly traditionalism which the peasant prized. Outside of, but symbolizing the wider universe in which the village functioned, was the magnificent capital city with its god-king.

The European world, when and where it impinged at all, was noticed largely in terms of minor technological improvements, a few consumers' goods, and a small share in the money economy of the outer world. European administrative and industrial enterprises were localized in new cities like Singapore, Batavia, or Rangoon. The missionary efforts on the whole were insignificant and, where their effect was felt at all, it was on the pagan fringes of the great Asian religions.

The second class indigenous to Southeast Asia when the Europeans came was the aristocracy. I shall dwell at some length on the old, the transitional, and the future role of this group because I consider them one of the major factors in the changes that have occurred in Southeast Asian culture. The old aristocracy lived by virtue of its symbolic role in the capital city, the symbol of the city of heaven, reigned over by a king whose exalted status in theory in no way spared him from the vicious intrigues and murderous rivalries of an idle court. Here was a class whose ethos was deeply at variance from that of the peasantry. It conceived of life in terms of hierarchy and power rather than in terms of simple communal democracy; in terms of privilege rather than mutual obligations; in terms of ostentation and aggrandizement rather than subsistence and communal obligations. But to both groups, religion, the capital city as symbol of the world order (however limited geographically their concept of the world), and the relationships between classes formed a deeply integrated and unquestioned cultural entity.

When Europeans began to apply themselves seriously to their colonial task in Southeast Asia, they worked largely through the courts and princely lines since, in the eighteenth century, these courts represented the only power centers of the area. They were also, on the surface at least, one of the few familiar landmarks to Europeans, who fully understood from their own culture the role of a king-aristocrat and the rules of power intrigue. Europeans entered into court life as tolerated eccentrics and minor advisors with a sharp eye for business. They were simply one variety of foreigner in courts which were exceptionally tolerant of cultural variations. The upper levels of society in the Far, Near, and Middle East in the seventeenth and eighteenth centuries had a much greater degree of contact with other cultures than Europe from its ethnocentric point of view then realized or even then enjoyed. Eccentricities of race, language, dress, and manner were taken with a sophisticated good humor in Southeast Asia which Europe at the end of the eighteenth century was only beginning to approximate and which it largely lost again in the nineteenth century.

First from the tolerance, and then from the cupidity of the Oriental ruling class, Europeans profited for three centuries. Once admitted to court circles, Europeans joined skillfully in the spirit of intrigue and oppression that pervaded them (however indignant certain good men may have been at the barbarous practices they witnessed). The symptoms, but not the system, were antipathetic to Europeans. But Europeans by degrees brought in their wake a superior technology, particularly in war. Gradually but persistently the courts of southern Asia became either the pawns of growing European interests or were liquidated by European nabobs in favor of direct political control.

As I pointed out earlier, the ethos of the Southeast Asian aristocracy differed from that of the peasant masses. The aristocracy existed by virtue of a value system which automatically accorded it power. With the growth of European interests this aristocracy found itself face to face with divergent values and a power greater than its own. It had only two choices: to ally itself with the impotent and unfamiliar masses or to adapt itself to the equally unfamiliar but obviously powerful Europeans. Undoubtedly many of the lower aristocracy sank into the anonymity of the peasantry. As a result the aristocracy we know today in Southeast Asia are the descendants of those who chose to adapt. The choice was neither astonishing nor, in those times and areas, despicable. Nationalism, as a loyalty to a politically defined area and people, is a European creation and until recently utterly unknown in southern Asia. Even in recent times and in areas where national sentiments are deeply rooted and highly valued, we have seen examples of groups of people who, feeling their status position threatened, seek support across national boundaries. The attitude of many Frenchmen toward Hitler Germany is a case still fresh in our minds. The European and American Communists who operate under orders from Russia are another instance.

The alliance of the Southeast Asian aristocracy with the Europeans took various forms. Their mutual economic benefit from the alliance was by no means the least of these. Politically the Europeans maintained a façade of indigenous forms. Deference was paid princelings: the sultans of Malaya were allowed to retain their courts, the sultan of

Jogjakarta his palace, his parasols, and his skirted soldiers. By these means the aristocracy in turn was able to retain a show of its old status prerogatives. In 1940 such sultans, radjahs, and princelings as were left had become museum pieces. They were as fine an example of a cultural lag as you will find anywhere.

Meanwhile, however, the aristocracy contributed also to a new indigenous upper-class group, the Europeanized intellectuals. Sons were sent to Europe for education. They learned English, French, or Dutch. More importantly they absorbed the social philosophies of nineteenth century Europe and transported to Southeast Asia European ideas which European colonials had not been at great pains to transmit. Therefore by 1940 the upper Asian class had split into the carefully preserved museum pieces on the one hand, and on the other, into the new intellectual group. This aspect of the class structure will be discussed later.

Meanwhile, let us return to the past. As we have said, Southeast Asia was an integrated culture, but a culture can be integrated around two or more goals. Southeast Asia had two such goals: the village communalism of the peasantry and the hierarchical system of the aristocracy. In the interstices of such a structure two new groups, the Europeans and the Chinese, had little difficulty in finding toe holds. For this situation I can detect at least two reasons: first, the original society itself had widely split class goals; and second, the objectives of the Europeans seemed at first so irrelevant as to present no threat to either of the pre-existing ones.

Although Chinese culture was one of the original formative strains in Southeast Asia, the Chinese for many centuries had had only a slightly less superficial political and commercial contact with Southeast Asia than the early European intruders had had. With the introduction of European colonialism, as opposed to commercialism, a new and much larger stream of Chinese migration into the area began. Today it is estimated that there must be some four and a half to six million Chinese in Southeast Asia. Many of these were imported as contract labor or came as small entrepreneurs after the advent of the Europeans. When Chinese laborers remained it was usually because they managed to promote their fortunes sufficiently to become themselves entrepreneurs. Europeans then imported more cheap Chinese labor to replace them. Today the Chinese in Southeast Asia are still split into these two groups. There are the landless wage earners on the one hand, and on the other, the moderately well-off, and occasionally very rich, entrepreneurs. One of the very striking characteristics of the Chinese community both at home and abroad is its upward mobility. The Chinese, in contrast to the other people in Southeast Asia, are always "getting ahead"—from coolies to small entrepreneurs, from small entrepreneurs to capitalists. In the course of this upward mobility they have moved constantly closer to the political, judicial, and economic privileges assumed by the European community—which was always on top and therefore could go no farther.

Economically these overseas Chinese are a source of considerable wealth to the homeland. Remittances flow steadily from Southeast Asia to China. Politically, the Chinese look to China even though they may have been resident in Southeast Asia for several generations. Nineteen representatives from Southeast Asia sit in the Chinese National Assembly. Further, the Chinese community has aligned itself politically in terms of the homeland with the result that Communist-Kuomintang feuds have been injected into a foreign political scene. Despite this political split within the Chinese community, it is still socially a solid group occupying an intermediary position in the wider framework of Southeast Asian class structure. The Chinese are sometimes referred to as the middle class. This may be a dangerously misleading analogy. There is little in common between the Chinese colonial in Southeast Asia today and the bourgeoisie of Europe, except that both have thriven and grown powerful between upper and lower millstones.

I should hasten to say that the overseas Chinese are not popular in Southeast Asia. On the one hand they are to some extent creatures of the European colonial system, and on the other hand their obsessive capacity for work outstrips even that of Europeans. Through their commercial shrewdness, through their persistence, and through their numbers they have not only swept up all the crumbs that have fallen from the rich profits of the introduced European economy, but they have also revealed character traits and life values not at all congenial to the indigenous peoples. Lastly, and perhaps most unforgivably, particularly in recent years, they have tenaciously remained a people apart in struggles for independence.

This brings us to a consideration of the European in the class structure of Southeast Asia. Class structure in its most rigid form may approximate a caste system. Among the criteria of caste is marriage within the group, characteristic occupations, and particularistic social observances which may range from food tabus to religious forms. This caste-like role was certainly that of Europeans not only in Southeast Asia but in most colonies established among the colored populations of the world. In Southeast Asia Europeans have existed, whether singly or in groups, above and apart, encysted, powerful, and inviolate. To the peasantry their status (if not their functions) must have seemed not too different from that which their own aristocracy had held for generations, but without the comprehensible system of unquestioned religious and traditional values to validate the assumption of such a status.

To summarize, the class structure of Southeast Asia in 1940 consisted of four major ethos groups: the peasantry and the aristocracy, which were indigenous; the caste-like European group; and an intermediary Chinese community, in itself split into the prosperous and conservative elements and the wage earners. Of these four elements two made very little pretense of being at home in the society into which they were transplanted. In terms of class structure, the old integration of Southeast Asian society had been at least shaken, but it failed to be destroyed because the intrusive elements insisted so vigorously upon their aloofness.

So schematic a discussion of class structure in Southeast Asia cannot be dropped without a few qualifying remarks. The impact of Europeans on the area has produced a small group of native wage earners drawn either from the peasantry or the lower reaches of the old aristocracy. There are also the unhappy and quite literally *declassé* Eurasians. There are the Indian coolies and the Indian and Arab moneylenders. None of these, however, either numerically or dynamically, play major roles in the class structure of most of the countries of Southeast Asia.

The economy of Southeast Asia has been implicit in much that has been said concerning class structure. Today, the peasantry feeds itself, the aristocracy, and the Chinese. In addition it has supplied in the last seventy-five years

through the good offices of the Chinese middlemen and colonial transportation systems, local food deficiency areas.
These areas of deficient food supply in southern Asia appear to have arisen as a by-product of the introduced European economic system. Burma, Siam, and Indochina before
the war had sufficient incentive goods and sufficient commercial organizations to be able to send almost six million
metric tons of rice primarily to adjacent areas but also to
the world at large. India on the other hand has been steadily impoverished in this respect for the last two hundred
and fifty years as the result of many sequences of interacting factors: the tremendous increases in population, the
growth of urban population in conjunction with the development of European enterprise, the system of land inheritance, and the disappearance of her own cottage industry.
India became a deficiency food area depending on the rice
surplus of Southeast Asia. Similarly Malaya, which was the
heart of European enterprise in Southeast Asia, did not raise
sufficient quantities of its own food to supply the imported
Chinese and Indian labor. Java's population, under an active policy of plantation exploitation in the nineteenth century, and in the twentieth century, under a highly conscientious public health administration, had reached a saturation
point in 1940. Only the most favorable coordination of administration, transportation, and technological improvements kept Java from food shortages.

But still in 1940 the peasant of Southeast Asia lived essentially in terms of subsistence economy, poorly, on his own
lands. In the older class system, his labor supported himself
and the idle, honored aristocracy. In 1940 it was contribut-
ing food, if not wealth, to imported populations, and to the
areas dislocated by the European colonial economy. His re-

40

wards for these additional burdens were unified political administration, some money with which to buy a few incentive goods, some public health services, a minimum of education, and a system of transportation and communication far more relevant to European needs than to his own.

However, by 1940 another system of economy was flourishing side by side with the indigenous economy based on small self-sufficient areas of approximately one hundred square miles. Europeans had introduced the plantation system whereby a number of highly profitable export crops were grown either by the local peasantry or by imported labor which worked for wages low enough to leave wide margins of profit. Before too many decades even the constantly expanding international markets were glutted, prices fell, an acute depression occurred, and commodity control agreements seemed indicated to maintain profits. The tropical soils and climate of Southeast Asia supported the production of rubber, sugar, coffee, tea, a variety of vegetable oils, spices, and a dozen other different commodities which Western Europe came to accept as not only luxuries but necessities. In addition there were tin, bauxite, and petroleum resources to develop. Last of all, of course, there were the local markets for consumers' goods manufactured in Europe, but unfortunately European capitalistic enterprise failed to establish, in time, that nice balance between what it was extracting from Southeast Asia and what it could put back into the area in the guise of purchasing power. It was defeated by its own preoccupation with what was proved to be, in the long run, uneconomical profit. In Southeast Asia technology could be allowed to lag behind that of Europe because local labor was cheaper than imported machinery. And when local labor proved inept or unmotivated there was always the inexhaustible and impoverished population of China and India. The result for the indigenous economy was becoming increasingly evident. Lands taken out of peasant cultivation for export crops in some countries were reducing areas available to a growing native population and simultaneously the need to feed imported labor was upsetting the native self-sufficiency pattern.

To the Chinese and to the Indians, but more especially to the Chinese, Southeast Asia was a land of milk and honey. The rows of coolie shacks, the small-scale mineral deposits, jungles which could be cleared for small plantations, the wealth of fish, the opportunities for small shopkeepers on the fringes of European settlements, were pledges of prosperity comparable perhaps to those of the West in our own pioneer traditions.

We have now sketched the establishment of a dual economy — the European colonial system as it coexisted with the persisting and functioning native system. We have seen that the economy of the original cultural integration, like the class structure, was shaken but by no means destroyed.

In this social and economic milieu there appeared the first signs of a new and reintegrative force at work in Southeast Asia, namely, the imported European philosophies.

From the late nineteenth century onward, there appeared for the first time in Southeast Asia some hints of a real diffusion of European values and goals. Ideas, as well as things, people, and systems, began to appear.

The new ideas brought from Europe by the native upper class derived chiefly from three European streams of thought: social humanism, nationalism, and Marxism.

The social humanistic ideas primarily took the form of emphasis on education (only it was education in local terms and not the transplanted, ill-adapted European system). It took the form of trade unionism but for local workers employed by European enterprise. And it took the form of legal safeguards but for the Southeast Asians. In other words there was introduced that most potent of all European ideals, the dignity of the individual — an idea so profound, so delicate, so human, that our own time and tradition is still struggling to implement it. (I should like to stress that the dignity of the individual is not identical with individualism.) Conscientious European administrators in Southeast Asia, prodded by the European-educated intellectuals of the area and by political scruples in the metropolitan countries of Europe, moved slowly forward to implement such ideas, despite resistance from European colonial commercial interests, which were already lagging behind Europe itself.

Chronologically, nationalism was the second idea imported from Europe. European nationalism has no relation to the old Southeast Asian idea of the state as a world order. It has therefore not immediately stimulated a return to the old pre-European order. In the nineteenth century Europeans devised the white man's burden as a rationalization of the inconsistency between nationalism as a positive virtue and the establishment of colonial empires. This rationalization fitted nicely into the theme of social humanism. Although European nationalism is as foreign as social humanism in Southeast Asia, it seems to have made more rapid and vigorous inroads than the latter, but both were accepted without colonialism as a concomitant. Probably very few Americans, and almost as few Europeans, realized prior to 1941 the strength with which these two European values had taken root in Southeast Asia. Only a part of the European administrators recognized the dilemma they were facing in running a colony and seeing the colonial peoples take seriously such European values. In other words, some of the internal inconsistencies of a not too well integrated European culture were being magnified in the colonial setting. The inconsistencies of the European theory and practice, and the spuriousness of the rationalization, showed up in high relief when transplanted. The choice was either the impossible task of muzzling the nationalist-humanist traditions at home and abroad, or a relaxation and modification of empire control. The vacillation of metropolitan powers in facing these inconsistencies in their colonies was, and is still today, one of the practical problems of statesmen. The United States was late in entering the Philippines, but, with varying strains upon its virtue and upon its self-interest, it recognized the dilemma and resolved it.

Marxism, the third great philosophic importation from Europe, entered Southeast Asia some three decades after social humanism and nationalism. It is important to realize that Marxism is not a theory based on cross-cultural data although it is so applied, and that it is as much a highly stylized example of Western thinking as social humanism and nationalism. Like so much of Western European contemporary philosophic and historical thinking about other cultures, it does not transcend our problems but merely tries to resolve Western European dilemmas and in the process universalizes them. On first inspection Marxism does appear to reconcile thesis and antithesis. Certainly Marxism appealed to some of the Southeast Asian intellectuals studying in Europe and grappling with the internal contradictions between nationalism and colonialism. It appealed also to the only Asian laboring group which had any appreciable contact with the Western world and the trade union movement — the seamen. Incidentally, these Asian seamen are a group so mentally alert to world crosscurrents that I am astonished to find for you no point of contact in popular literature other than Mr. Kipling's references to lascars and their rascally habits.

Russia, meanwhile (and that means primarily from the time of the Russian Revolution until Trotsky's exile) had been actively and very practically proselytizing and educating leadership for the world revolution not only in Southeast Asia but in all Asia. Marxism therefore was greatly strengthened (1) by its apparent reconciliation of social humanism and nationalism in colonial areas; (2) by its appeal to two entirely different groups of Southeast Asians, the intellectuals and the seamen; and (3) by the practical efforts of Russia, which in the 1920's was still a revolutionary nation. Marxian philosophy, sociology, and economics made a strong appeal to the numerically small but vigorous groups in Southeast Asia which were searching to create a new integration out of their own native traditions and European cultural impacts.

There are undoubtedly many other aspects of European thought systems which began to filter into Southeast Asia during this period. Political democracy was one of them. The existence and importance of international relations was another. The potency of technology and of capital in the modern world was a third. But more important than all these ideas, it seems to me, was a new sense of the speed of cultural changes, the acceleration of social life in the twentieth century. This realization bit deeply into the consciousness of the new Southeast Asian leaders. Their traditionalism, gradualism, and patience were foreshortened from centuries to decades. In turn, as this concept permeates to the Southeast Asian peoples, traditionalism will loose its hold. Perhaps this, in the last analysis, is the greatest revolution in the area.

In this combination that we have been describing of shaken class structure, of a dual economy, and of the infiltration of European philosophic values, the important but elusive question of prestige remains to be examined.

Where a mixed class structure exists, it would be brash to suppose that prestige necessarily parallels hierarchy. In Southeast Asia, prestige has been as fragmented as the class structure and the economy.

Naturally the Europeans had few doubts, consciously at least, that they stood at the top of the prestige system. Next down the line in European eyes came the local aristocracy and the wealthy Chinese, then the middle-class Chinese and Eurasians; next the imported coolie labor, and last of all the indigenous peasantry. On the whole the Chinese acquiesced to this European system of prestige ratings. Needless to say, the Southeast Asians did not. The old aristocracy, however humble in their behavior, never lost the sense of their own innate superiority. The peasantry meanwhile continued to support the aristocrats' attitude with unquestioning loyalty. For example, in the Europeanized cities, house servants who were themselves a sort of white-collar group, felt infinitely more pride in serving one of their own aristocracy than in serving a European — even though the pay might not be so good and even though the aristocrat served might be lower in the governmental hierarchy than the European. Service in a Chinese family was still less desirable than in a European.

The question of prestige, intangible and elusive as it is, is nevertheless of great importance because it is one of the guides to the values cherished by the culture. And in respect to values, between Southeast Asian and European, no two more contrasting sets of ideas as to what constitutes the "fitting," the "admirable," the "desirable," could well be found. The European — and the American — admires individualism, initiative, change, and what he calls progress. His character structure is generally competitive and acquisitive. At home, his class structure is distinguished by upward mobility. The Southeast Asian, in the past at least, prized conformity, quiescence, stability, traditionalism. The European esteems the man who pulls himself up by his own bootstraps (even though he may sometimes offend good taste in the process). The Southeast Asian admires the man of birth and innate breeding. Europeans feel that plain speaking, a touch of iron, and a bit of anger are useful devices in getting your own way. The Southeast Asian prefers and admires the subtle and indirect approach. He prizes equanimity. A loud voice, bluntness, and anger are vulgar. They are the standard characteristics of the buffoons in their traditional drama. Fat bodies and round eyes are gross. Physical exertion and sweat are for the lowest groups. A slim physique, reserve, a low thin voice, oblique eyes, graceful, restrained, flowing gestures — these are the marks of a man worthy of being accorded respect.

I recall with more than a little sympathy the spectacle of an earnest young Dutch administrator, tall, heavy-limbed, blond, and blue eyed, cantering madly down a road, throwing himself in a sweat from his horse, and shouting angrily at some craftsmen who were proving both slow and inept in building his house. The poor man was beside himself with heat and frustration; he was beyond belief vulgar and ludicrous. Even the frightened and obsequious native carpenters found it hard to conceal their delight in so amusing a display of what constitutes buffoonery in their own dramatic tradition. A native aristocrat under circumstances arousing a comparable degree of anger might have turned away and quietly ordered an underling to flog the offenders.

One other element remains to be appraised in this situation — the growing dislike and the growing awareness of Europeans by Southeast Asians in the first four decades of the twentieth century. So long as the European existed in an undisturbed society, so long as he remained a remote and obscure person, who impinged upon only a very few in the area, his calm assumption of a caste-like superiority was not disturbing to the mass of the people. But Europeans began to arrive in greater numbers as enterprises were enlarged and as administration was extended. Opportunities to observe Europeans at close range increased. The Southeast Asians began to encounter the European petit bourgeois with his cultural predilections heavy upon him. He saw the caste system intensified as European women arrived to set up their own society and to raise their children. Discrepancies not only became more obvious; they became more acute. The Southeast Asians were beginning to absorb ideas of social humanism and of nationalism; in addition they had their own great sense of what constituted personal dignity; they had no traditional values by which to rationalize the presence of Europeans in their midst comparable to traditions which rationalized the presence of their aristocracy. They did not like what they saw.

All the socially disintegrative forces previously mentioned were finding expression in emotional tensions which were felt by both sides—and how keenly one needed only to travel in the area prior to the war to sense.

Where the Chinese stand in this picture of the valued person, I do not know. I can only impart the impression that their humor, their shrewd, materialistic appraisal of life, their conviction of superiority so deep that it is unnecessary to manifest it in crude form, has made them at least somewhat acceptable to many Europeans. I doubt, however, that they are intermediary in the range of values present in Southeast Asia in the way they are in class position and economic function. I suspect that they possess an entirely different value complex. But these matters are subject only to speculation based on the consensus of knowledgeable persons. The necessary grass-root studies of cultural dynamics remain to be made.

This, then, in generalized terms was the status of forces arrayed for and against a new world in Southeast Asia in approximately the decade from 1930 to 1940.

Then came the Japanese invasion. Where violence prevails, reason, constructive philosophies, and patience have a way of fading before the force of negative emotions. The Southeast Asians were at first either indifferent to or pleased and relieved by the defeat of the European colonial system and its disappearance from the scene. The fall of Singapore, the capitulation at Bandoeng, the retreat in Burma appear to have been viewed with fatalistic or complacent eyes by most Southeast Asians.

Of course there were exceptions. The Chinese, who had been at war with Japan for five years and whose politics were those of China (rather than Europe), aided resistance at the time of conquest and later, to the best of their ability and so long as the sacrifices, of at least the wealthy, were not too great. The Filipinos were another Southeast Asian people among whom the percentage identifying themselves with the European democracies ran high. The causes in the case of the Filipinos were diverse: first, Spanish missionary labors in the Philippines for three hundred years had led to a higher degree of acculturation; secondly, the United States had pursued toward the Philippines a generous educational and political policy; thirdly, Americans remained to fight with Filipinos at Bataan; and fourthly, independence had been promised them.

On the whole the thin crust of local leadership in Southeast Asia broke up into various factions with the Japanese invasion. There were those who saw in the Japanese an Asian deliverer; there were those who saw only an opportunity to advance nationalistic interests during the conflict; and lastly, there were those who saw Japan clearly in world affairs as a weak yet dangerous manifestation of nationalistic fervor carried to a logical but to them shocking extreme.

But, by 1943, it was already apparent that whatever advantages the Japanese may have had in the minds of the Southeast Asians at the time of the conquest, they were being dissipated for two major reasons. First, Japan was economically impotent in the area. After preliminary looting of supplies needed for Japanese stock piles, there were neither shipping nor incentives to maintain Southeast Asia's colonial economy. Even those small surpluses which accrued to the local population in the shape of consumers' goods gradually disappeared from the market. With very few adjustments the majority of the Southeast Asian peoples were able to return to their original subsistence economy and cottage industries. This return to their own devices was undoubtedly psychologically reassuring. The second reason for Japan's loss of those advantages it had at the time of the conquest was a psychological ineptitude which exceeded even that of the colonial Europeans. Boastfulness, violence, and deception, the wholesale removal of men for labor corps, all served to alienate the Southeast Asians with astonishing rapidity.

This chapter has characterized briefly the nature of cultural integration in Southeast Asia prior to the period of intensive European colonization particularly in respect to class structure and the economic system. We have touched upon some of the social and cultural impacts of Europe which shook or stimulated Southeast Asian countries without on the whole genuinely destroying their integration. We have looked at some of the discrepant values of Europeans and Southeast Asians, and have seen them reinforcing a growing emotional tension between the two groups. Japan's occupation of the area served to confirm the repudiation of Europeans without enhancing the reputation of the Japanese.

Chapter III

POTENTIALITIES OF THESE FACTORS

THE Japanese conquest of Southeast Asia failed to stir enthusiasm for the Japanese, and for their version of the Co-Prosperity Sphere and of Greater East Asia in the minds of the peoples of those countries. The war, however, did accentuate nationalist sentiments and the determination to achieve independence. First, Japan granted at least the illusion of independence to the Burmese, the Laotians, Cambodians, and the Filipinos; and at the time of capitulation sanctioned the formation of the Republic of Indonesia and the Vietnam in Indochina. During the war a second source of encouragement to independence was the Atlantic Charter and the formation of a United Nations Organization in San Francisco. To Southeast Asians news of these two pledges were heard over short-wave radio sets at the risk of reprisal. Promises concerning the autonomy of dependent peoples were accepted with deep trust and literalness.

In addition to nationalism the immediate aftermaths of V-J day accentuated another tendency present before the war in Southeast Asia. It was a tendency which the rapid capitulation of Western powers in the winter of 1941-42 had reinforced, namely, loss of prestige for Europeans. Before the war the European colonials may not have been held in high esteem, but at least their assumption of power went unquestioned by the man in the street and field. During and immediately after the war, neither power nor prestige were available to bolster European colonial claims in Southeast Asia.

In most areas, at least a month elapsed after V-J day before European military forces were able to return and even to accept the Japanese surrender. When they did appear, it was in small and unimpressive units, with none of the pomp and panoply which symbolizes authority to the Asian. Still more damaging was that the bulk of the fighting men who returned were not European but Indian troops. In addition, among the returning Europeans the great majority were the very individuals associated with the pre-war colonial regime. Last in this series of perhaps unavoidable but completely damaging events, the hated Japanese were charged in some areas by the Allied high command to maintain peace and order often, in opposition to native forces, until Allied military governments could take over. In certain cases the Japanese continued these functions for six months or longer. Parenthetically, it should be stated that many impartial observers spoke highly of the correctness and propriety with which the Japanese Army behaved under the circumstances and the degree to which Japanese face was restored thereby.

The irony of both the war and the immediate aftermath of the surrender could not, and did not, escape the people of Southeast Asia. Before the war, power had maintained the colonial regime despite growing tensions. The regimes were never accorded spontaneous allegiance. But the colonial power was shattered by the Japanese conquest. Nationalist sentiments were encouraged during the occupation of Southeast Asia both by the Japanese and by the pledges

53

of the Allies. Japanese land forces were not defeated in direct combat in Southeast Asia. After V-J day the ineptitudes of military reoccupation destroyed what power and prestige the Allies might have been accorded by the capitulation of Japan.

There seems little doubt that the metropolitan powers were faced with the need for political readjustments in Southeast Asia. This adjustment is coming either with good grace as in Burma, grudgingly and legalistically as in Indonesia, or accompanied by bitter fighting as in Indochina. At the moment nationalism in Southeast Asia is not only a positive political conviction; it is also a symbol of the deep emotional rejection of metropolitan Europeans as a superior caste. Both the people and their leaders are united in at least the negative determination not to accept their old masters on the old terms. The more grudging the metropolitan adjustment, the more intense will be the hostility engendered against Europeans. In long range terms Great Britain seems to be taking the most constructive role. The hatred which the French show of arms is creating in Indochina endangers not only France's economic and political future in the area, but in addition is fostering all the negative and destructive aspects of relations between Southeast Asians and Europeans. In a wider frame it weakens all relationships between the democracies and the so-called dependent peoples of the world. For a limited period of time the Southeast Asian moderates will recognize the need for support and will be willing to turn to the metropolitan countries for it. If they find there no genuine appreciation of their aspirations, they will either be discredited in the eyes of their own people or may turn elsewhere for the assistance they avowedly need.

This is the present and unhappy state of affairs in Southeast Asia. In the preceding chapter it was suggested that the integration of Southeast Asian cultures had been shaken by colonialism and that they had also received in the process a series of new values and an acceleration in the tempo of change. They have been made aware of the outside world and in the process have become more conscious of themselves and their own cultural predilections. It may be profitable to speculate upon the form which new integrations of Southeast Asia may take, both in terms of its internal values and its external relations should that area be permitted to choose its own course.

The first vital change to be anticipated in Southeast Asia derives from the great increase in population. The relation of population growth to cultural change and to cultural integration is a problem recognized but not resolved. Asia is still at the beginning of a period of population growth which in Europe is ending. If we may analogize from Europe for lack of comparative data, a sevenfold increase in Asians may be expected before birth rates and declining death rates stabilize. Whether or not these same proportions work out precisely in Asia as they have in Europe, we can expect that two centuries hence there will be an even greater disproportion between Asians and Europeans than now exists.

These population increases will serve, at least indirectly, as forces to alter economic and political patterns. How and in what direction these forces will manifest themselves in the long run is a research field of major importance now and for the next generations. However, some repercussions may be suggested. It seems unlikely that population growths will be adjusted by migrations. It is more likely that local leadership will stress technological improvements and industrial development. If such developments do not keep pace with population, revolutionary ideologies will find fertile breeding grounds. Also as population grows, whether or not it is increasingly poverty stricken, the political demands of these areas will become more insistent.

On a narrower time scale intellectual, political, and economic forces shaping the next two decades are more easily discernible.

Intellectually the changes that may be expected in the next generation in Southeast Asian countries are both an eager but inept copying of Western forms and a pedantic perpetuation of their own classical traditions. The copying of Western forms can be expected in all art media and in the field of thought. We can expect quantitatively great vigor. I suspect, however, that, qualitatively, the works of art will seem to Europeans stiff, unskilled, and lifeless; the intellectual productions will reflect generalized and abstract tendencies. The simultaneous return to old forms will serve as a reaction to this ill-absorbed and slavish westernism. Sterile copies and craftsmanly reproductions of past glories in the arts are to be anticipated. Intellectual rejection of westernisms will undoubtedly manifest itself in scholarly commentaries on classical literature and the placing of undue value on local languages. In sum, we may expect a neo-classicism on the one hand and a poor imitation of the West on the other hand.

Then under favorable circumstances a genuine renascence might be expected. Those who wish to gauge how rapidly and in what direction the reintegration of Southeast Asian culture is going should watch closely the changes in the intellectual and artistic life of the area. Because our knowledge of the intimate processes at work in Southeast Asia today is so faulty, the time and nature of a renascence cannot be predicted. Because the barriers of language and cross-cultural comprehensions are so great, we shall be tempted to neglect this field. Yet its symptomatic importance will be no wise minimized because we Westerners promise to be incompetent in coping with it.

Let us now continue with an area of change in which we, as Westerners, feel ourselves more competent and in which we, therefore, have greater interest. I refer to the political changes that can be anticipated and the social structuring associated with such changes.

Politically the countries of Southeast Asia are today committed first of all to their independence. This is a direct expression of the new nationalism. However, there is frequently a wide gap between theory and practice, and cultural lags are a common phenomenon, particularly in societies undergoing rapid changes. Europe shows some evidence of lagging behind its own best theory and practice in relation to colonial areas. For Southeast Asia the result of the gap between theory and practice on the one hand, and of Europe's lag in applying its theory to colonies on the other hand, will mean that instead of freedom for national experiments in Southeast Asian countries, various forms of self-government and internal autonomy within a framework of a European-dominated union will be offered. The formulas presented by the Kingdom of the Netherlands, which is to include the United States of Indonesia with the constituent Republic of Indonesia, or the French Union with its Federation of Indochina, or of "Sovietism," are cases in point.

Politically the Southeast Asian countries are committed to independence. They are less committed to republicanism which seems in Europe, at least, to have depended on a prosperous and politically competent middle class. Our statesmen should be encouraged, but not carelessly optimistic, that constitutional forms of government have been phrased in the last three years by Indonesia, Malaya, Vietnam, and Burma; that Siam already has its constitutional monarchy; and that the Philippines with their experience during the commonwealth period behind them, were well prepared to implement democratic political forms.

Republicanism has implied in all these areas the almost immediate enfranchisement of the masses. This in turn has lent a new acuteness to the need for literacy. The claimed achievements of the Vietnam in both extending the franchise and extending literacy during elections in January 1946 were remarkable (if true) and a token of what can be done. The Annamese claim to have gained two and a half million literates in their drive and to have set a goal of six million. Siam also claims to have raised her literacy level from 31 percent to 48 percent of the population during the last ten years. With the assistance of the United States the literacy of the Philippines is now probably about 48 percent of her population. One is tempted to assume that literacy is positively correlated with the degree of political autonomy made available to an area.

In connection with the growth of new political forms, a point raised in the last chapter deserves attention. The split in the old aristocracy produced by European expansion and the adaptive capacity which the aristocracy showed in the face of that pressure was mentioned. The receptivity of the aristocracy resulted in its breaking up into one group of carefully preserved museum pieces, and another group which has contributed to the new intellectual and Europeanized upper class. The radjahs, the princelings, the sultans, represent a cultural lag whose role, quite unwittingly, has been to preserve in the peasantry the old respect for its rulers. Today that respect may be available for reinterpretation and transfer to the intellectual upper class. Such a transference would not only be easy for the masses, but would be acceptable to the upper class itself. This, however, may well be only an interim phenomenon since leadership is preaching a political doctrine that contains the seed of its own decay. If the new leadership persists in implementing ideas of political democracy, with literacy and the franchise as its necessary concomitants, then Southeast Asia may well be on the verge of revolutionary culture changes stimulated in the first place by external contacts but now promising to be worked out in terms of internal forces.

When Europeans undermined the genuine position of the old aristocracy, they initiated chain reactions which will in all probability unleash the political effectiveness of the peasant masses. If culture is an integrated phenomenon as postulated in the first chapter, then we must assume that altering one set of institutions or values will be felt throughout the society. If the Western democracies desire a republican form of government, attendant changes must be anticipated.

In time the intellectual upper class will undoubtedly lose their status as a class apart — and with it the prestige inherited from the old aristocracy. The aristocratic class, which the European influence did much to weaken, as well as the intellectuals who were its heirs, will eventually receive its *coup de grâce* from the people itself. When that time comes, the cultures of Southeast Asia will be ready to reintegrate themselves either in new terms which we cannot now foresee, or they will pattern themselves on one or the other of the European stereotypes now current. For the present, it is important to remember that their choices may not be dictated solely by the alternatives which seem to face contemporary European culture.

Obviously even this theoretic possibility will not be achieved in a year or a decade. In the interim the old ethos will survive, prestige and status will continue to be granted the upper and European-educated class which is now replacing the old aristocracy. This group can be expected to rule, to intrigue, to manipulate the wealth of their country with different techniques but with much the same power goals as the older colonial and pre-colonial ruling cliques. The educated upper class will not only inherit the respect accorded the old aristocracy but will maintain for a time its ruling functions.

It would be unrealistic to expect that the Southeast Asian countries will burgeon overnight into governments with two-party or multi-party systems. There will not immediately appear a tradition of disinterested public service. Nor can it be anticipated that there will be immediately a high-minded bureaucracy serving the people. That such a pattern is unlikely to develop overnight is already evinced by the course of Siamese and Philippine politics. What we can realistically expect are one-party governments. Within these single parties the cliques, largely phrased in terms of personal loyalties, will form and break off; there will be *coups d'états* in which personnel will switch but not fundamental objectives.

The Western democracies may then yield to the temptation of finger-pointing and name-calling of either the fascist or communist variety since in European society these have been the outstanding varieties of one-party governments. I am convinced, however, that this would represent just another error in easy analogizing that we so often fall into when dealing with foreign cultures. The most superficial resemblance leads us into mistaking the part for the whole.

In the near future, in let us say the next decade, we should expect the disappearance of that unity which now binds the leadership of many of these countries that are emerging from colonialism. The reason is not far to seek and has been repeatedly stated. Nationalism as a force in the cultures of the area is new and has not yet a genuine integration. Its present vigor is largely a manifestation of resistance to the inequities and humiliations of the colonial system. The leaders of the present nationalism stem from a variety of schools of political philosophy and undoubtedly possess varying degrees of personal integrity, of vision, of sophistication, and of the old aristocratic ethos. As pressure from Europe is relaxed and the present crisis is replaced by some form of more or less stable government, the internal differences between leaders are bound to assert themselves. Only the most destructive and ungenerous policies on the part of Western democracies, combined with a vigorous introduced leadership and propaganda from Russia, could distort into totalitarianism as we have known it in Europe the inevitable but traditional one-party rule of the young Southeast Asian countries.

Nazi totalitarianism and racial hatreds have become synonymous to Europeans. If the label of totalitarianism is attached to Southeast Asian nations, the racist accusations will follow easily. Already, resistance in these countries to the return of colonial systems has been represented as being anti-white. It has been claimed that the real purpose of the extremists is to kill off white men or women who dare to show their faces in the area hereafter. Certainly guilt about

61

racial problems, reinforced by recent political experiences with Germany, make such a projection a natural one. Fuel was added to our own deep uneasiness and guilt on the score of racial discrimination by the Japanese slogan of Asia for the Asians and by the Japanese drive to humiliate European prisoners before Asian peoples.

However, in Southeast Asia there is little to support such assumptions. The clearly stated policies of moderate Southeast Asian leaders reiterate their willingness to cooperate economically and diplomatically with Europeans. The prestige of Americans could scarcely have been higher than it was at V-J day in Southeast Asia. The record of Southeast Asians toward European internees and prisoners of war was not that of racial fanatics. There is nothing in the cultural background, in the emotional constitution, or in the actual record which substantiates such accusations. They appear to stem, instead, from projection mechanisms of our own.

Southeast Asia is more concerned with social and political problems than with economic ones, not because economic questions are not pressing but because it is not, like Western Europe, a culture of acquisitive and competitive individuals with a highly complex rationale of this value. On the contrary, the traditional patterns are essentially non-acquisitive. Yet the need to take a place in the modern world of industrial change and international trade is not overlooked in the area. The economic reintegration of Southeast Asian cultures will undoubtedly be in the direction of state socialism — if left to their own devices. This state socialism is, however, another theory that can be expected to fall far short of practice. For one thing, the only extensive industrial, agricultural, or mining holdings are European-owned. It is unlikely that any political settlement with present metropolitan powers would permit their confiscation. On the contrary, all the moderate leaders in the countries of Southeast Asia have already restored or promise to restore, or make due compensation for, such properties. The reasons are not only political, they are also directly referable to lack of local capital and technological skills. The restoration of these enterprises would furnish not only much needed foreign credits but also a profitable source of taxation.

The Southeast Asian countries may establish state-controlled industries but for many decades these will probably be limited to new industries and principally to the production of consumer goods and to public utilities. Available labor, capital, and materials would not support more ambitious schemes. But for even such modest schemes there is every indication that capital and guidance will be welcome from whatever sources so long as they are not exclusively from former metropoles and are not monopolistic. While such enterprises are being developed, the agricultural emphasis of Southeast Asian economy will undoubtedly be retained. And simultaneously plans will be made for state irrigation and power projects, since the present undeveloped condition of power resources is one of the great handicaps to industrial development in the area, and since expanded and improved irrigation is essential to the maintenance of a growing agricultural population. It is also probable that cottage industries will be encouraged during the period of readjustment. Lastly, it seems likely that cooperatives, particularly credit and marketing cooperatives aimed at breaking the hold of the Chinese middlemen, will flourish.

All these devices will serve neither to achieve pure state socialism nor essentially to end the system of dual economy. They will also not serve to meet the pressures of a growing population. I suspect that we shall see no cultural creativeness in the fashion in which the Southeast Asian nations tackle economic problems. Their genius does not lie in that direction. I imagine also that for a long time the politically powerful group will be disproportionately wealthy and that a considerable portion of their wealth may be invested abroad rather than at home if these countries stay within the sphere of Western democracies.

This very weakness in economic genius will undoubtedly attract European nations which are economically distressed. Although some of the most profitable exports have been developed elsewhere or substitutes found during the war, the European impulse is to return to pre-established patterns of behavior and to plan for the future in terms of extrapolation rather than in terms of new forces. Southeast Asia was and still is a low pressure area. Economically its resources have only been tapped. Internally the situation is not propitious for economic self-development. Our problem will be to learn to deal bi-laterally with peoples who have no pleasure in acquiring our competitive and acquisitive ways. It is even conceivable that we ourselves will learn in the next decades to move more in the direction of cooperative attitudes in order to achieve higher levels of human welfare. We may learn to see that the transfer of European ideas of individualism and competitive enterprise were wisely resisted in southern Asia and that they need less re-education for a role in one world than we do.

Although Southeast Asian countries are not likely to develop a high level of economic aggression, and although the present industrial nations of Europe may not for some time assert themselves with the same economic vigor they showed in the early twentieth century, we must nevertheless anticipate that Europeans will continue to be interested in influencing the development of Southeast Asia and that Japanese industry will not remain at the 1946 level. However, these influences will have to be exerted in a less politically propitious atmosphere than they were prior to the war at the same time that the need of economic readjustment becomes steadily more acute.

European intrusions in the area will be toned down leaving the region freer to receive the influences from other directions. Australia, for example, is not unaware of its Asian neighbors. Although it is still firmly attached to the sterling bloc and the system of Empire preferences both by necessity and sentiment, it is not closing its eyes to the possibility of new markets. At the moment, Australia is looking to Siam and Malaya but particularly to India, all of which are still within the same circle of economic necessity, if not within the same circle of sentimental preferences. Trade commissions to India have been exchanged since the war and their reports are immeasurably more sanguine than similar ones in the mid-1930's. Australia's Labor government has experienced difficulties in maintaining strict neutrality between the Dutch and the Indonesians in the face of the strikes of its pro-Indonesian Waterfront Workers Union. Australia realizes as never before how close geographically it is to the vast populations of Asia, how deep the ferment among these peoples is, how intimately its military security is linked to events in Asia, and how weak and distant Great Britain now seems.

But the hurdles facing Australia in any attempt to play a significant role in the region are tremendous. Australia is an offshoot of the expansionistic tradition of European culture which is becoming suspect in southern Asia. Its people are by and large a compact, urbanized, and liberal middle class. It has vigorously established a very high standard of living in part by keeping its population small. This effort has included the so-called White Australia policy as a bulwark against Asian encroachment. Whatever the advantage of such policies and practices to Australians, they form no easy bridge to winning the confidence of south Asians. Australia is a Far Eastern but not an Asian nation. Furthermore, its small population cannot absorb considerable proportions of the Southeast Asian exports any more than its industry is prepared to furnish the needed quantities of cheap consumer goods. At best a sympathetic Australia might serve as the last bridge between old stimuli and a new integration. Certainly Australia's vigorous post-war foreign policy has included championing the rights of small nations and of non-self-governing peoples.

India, on the other hand, stands highest in leadership potentials in Southeast Asia. However complex and demanding its own internal adjustments, the Indian leaders are determined to take a leading role in world and particularly in south Asian affairs. Their pronouncements and their acts in the last three years can leave no doubt in anyone's mind as to their intentions. Indian leaders have addressed themselves with particular sympathy to the struggles for independence now being waged in the Southeast Asian countries. India's own experience and its success in the struggle for autonomy, in the establishment of at least nascent industrial resources, in planning for the liquidation of poverty, in devising education for leadership, are being watched with interest in Southeast Asia. These examples may serve both as inspirations and models. The old Hinduistic cultural ties have been stressed both in India and Indonesia. The sympathy between the Indonesian and the well-disciplined Indian troops which occupied Java for a year escaped no one's notice. India's first foreign loan was to Siam in order to encourage trade between the two countries.

Economically, however, India has been in no better position than Australia since the end of the war to assist her Southeast Asian neighbors. But the sympathy, the growing power, the basic kinship, has been stressed. The aspirations for independence which have been rebuffed by the metropolitan powers and, until recently, ignored by the USSR would probably turn to an Asian nation were one effective enough to help solve their problems.

I need scarcely stress that I have been discussing a sentiment pattern, no more. The Southeast Asians have not liked Indians as cheap labor and as moneylenders any more than they have liked the Chinese. Usually international amity begins with reassuring pronouncements. Whether these courtship devices stabilize into a successful marriage depends on genuine mutuality. Whether India is to become again, after almost a millenium and a half, a cultural leader in Southeast Asia, will depend on issues a few of which are now identifiable. First, India must itself achieve political stability. Secondly, India's masses must not swamp Southeast Asia. That they will appears unlikely for two reasons. India's peasantry is not ordinarily highly migrant. It is as attached to its own landscape as were the Japanese. Another reason is that the future internal economic and political development of Southeast Asia is not likely to foster the immigration of cheap labor to the degree which it did in the full blush of colonial development. Economically, it will not be able to afford it. Politically, it will be too concerned in setting its own house in order.

67

If India is to become a leader in Southeast Asian affairs, another issue it will have to meet is its ability to lend genuine economic assistance in competition with Europe. This will not be easy despite the economic impoverishment of Europe and its geographic remoteness. India itself has so great and so urgent a problem in raising its own standard of living, in supplying its own shortages, in training its own educators and technicians, that it seems unlikely that it will have either manpower, capital, or materials to spare. However, it is likely that India will make every effort to advance capital and to spare consumers' goods in return for Southeast Asia's rice, tin, and petroleum.

A third area of potential leadership for India in southern Asia is in the field of international relations both within the framework of the United Nations and within the framework of an Asian bloc. In these two areas India has already shown not only idealistic vigor but a higher degree of astuteness than any other Asian nation. Indian leaders are exerting every effort even in the face of tremendous internal difficulties to meet the leaders of Southeast Asian countries and to encourage conferences of all kinds for a discussion of common problems. The Inter-Asian Conference, held in New Delhi in March 1947, may well presage a new direction in south Asian relationships.

The third great Far Eastern country which borders the low pressure area of Southeast Asia and which might assume an expansive interest in the area is China. Two decades ago, or even one, China's interest in Southeast Asia was again keen and growing. This interest was the source of much watchful concern to European nations. Today such interest although undoubtedly alive in China is largely ineffectual. Its civil war in size and bitterness is consuming

68

both political and economic energies. Neither participant in that war exemplifies the type of enlightened liberalism which appeals to the European-trained intellectuals of Southeast Asia. The renewed flood of immigrant Chinese into Southeast Asia is jeopardizing whatever position one or the other of the Chinese factions might take. Legally and illegally the Chinese are again moving into Southeast Asia, where opportunities seem greater than at home. The unpopularity of the Chinese in Southeast Asia was discussed in an earlier chapter. They are meeting the resistance born of their role as tools of the European colonial economy, of their own acquisitive vigor, of their unwillingness to assimilate culturally, of their imported political factionalism, and of their indifference to the national aspirations of their Southeast Asian hosts.

Unless unsuspected miracles occur in China itself and in the attitudes of the Chinese toward Southeast Asia, it seems highly improbable that China's political, economic, or cultural leadership will assert itself in the area for many years to come, or before Southeast Asian cultures are well on the way to their own reintegrations.

Are there then any nations, other than India, whose leadership in Southeast Asia may be expected to develop in the next decades?

Siam, the only Southeast Asian nation that has maintained its political independence during the colonial period might be theoretically, at least, a candidate. For the moment, however, Siam appears to have remained the most aloof of its neighbors to the affairs of the region. It seems engrossed in its traditional diplomatic role of balancing off the interest which the great powers have evinced in the country. The anomalous role of Siam during the war with

Japan has heightened its concern for restoring its position in the eyes of the Allies. Siam concentrated on admission to the United Nations as a symbol of its good intentions and peacefulness. Conciliatory gestures toward France, USSR, and China have all had to be made without loosening the hold which the ruling group has on the internal affairs of the country. These activities, intensified by tremendous inflation and the attendant corruption of public life, seem so to have engrossed Siam's attention that its relations to other south Asian neighbors remind one almost of the isolationist policies the United States used to pursue. However, Bangkok is at present the crossroads of the region, and it should not be forgotten that Siam's current indifference may alter if circumstances and time prove such a change expedient.

The Philippines are now the only other independent country of Southeast Asia which, again theoretically, might be expected to offer some leadership in the area. Certainly there have been strong unofficial statements of sympathy for the colonial areas of Southeast Asia and there have been unofficial discussions among Filipinos of a Federation of Southeast Asia. There has been talk, but only talk, of a Pan-Malayan Union. However, such comments have been so weak and sporadic that any likelihood of their implementation seems improbably remote. The emphasis on the Malayan element is also so partial as to alienate Burma, Siam, and Indochina.

But more formative than such considerations are the facts of the Philippines' orientation in both economic and international relations toward the United States. Leadership in the Philippines has recognized clearly and overtly that its material welfare and military security are dependent on good relations with the United States. International relationships can be expected to reflect these necessities.

The USSR's possible role in Southeast Asia is colored in the minds of most of us by its role in other parts of the world and by fears of conspiratorial techniques. Certainly Marxism and also Communism have been accepted by some of the Southeast Asian leaders who are now struggling for a greater or lesser measure of political freedom. Men like Ho Chi Minh of Indochina are frank to state that nationalism is only a stage, but at least they insist that it is a necessary and inevitable one. There seems to me, however, a wide gap between the presence of nationalists of Marxian persuasion and the presence of active conspiratorial groups of Soviet Communists. It appears to me that whether or not such a group does expand both in numbers and influence will depend largely on how rapidly the area reaches economic, political, and cultural stability in locally acceptable terms. Communist leadership fattens on poverty, unrest, and discontent. If the USSR is to make a lasting impact on Southeast Asia, it would have to be not only in terms of a few highly disciplined leaders and an ideology, but also in terms of practical suggestions for mass education, industrial development, and constructive handling of primitive minorities, in providing the necessary capital goods and technicians for establishing consumer goods industries. In none of these practical matters has the USSR shown initiative so far. Until recently, the USSR has even been weak in offering political and propagandic support to Southeast Asia. There has been, of course, some discrediting of the metropolitan countries, but it is obvious that the USSR lacks experts on the area. The raising of the Indonesian question in the United Nations by the Ukraine was phrased more for the purpose of embarrassing the British than helping the Indonesians. It came at the very time when Indonesians realized that the presence of the British was giving them an opportunity to negotiate with the Dutch. It only resulted in Sjahrir's repudiation of such assistance. However, since that time the USSR policy in support of colonial peoples is more clearly articulated and implemented. In 1948 the stereotypes of Europeans, whether eastern or western, and the aspirations of non-self-governing peoples are seen in sharper relief.

The discussion so far has stressed that European intrusions have not been popular. The opinion has been offered that Southeast Asia is on the verge of new integration which it is eager to work out, not in isolation, but in its own terms. Lastly, in running quickly over some of the nations which are prepared by cultural and geographic affinities as well as political and economic potentialities to expand into Southeast Asia, India most nearly fits the bill.

The role which various nations might play in the future within Southeast Asia has been examined cursorily. The role which Southeast Asian cultures may themselves play in the new international scene is worth consideration.

First, we can be assured that the countries of Southeast Asia will be enthusiastically international in their thinking. This attitude can be attributed to a number of factors. First, their sovereignty will be weak and they will seek fair and dispassionate protection in political, economic, and military fields. Second, their nationalism is still shallow and therefore any surrender of national sovereignty in the interest of international security will seem less crippling than it does to some of the states where nationalism is older and more deeply ingrained. Third, they have practically no external vested interests to protect either materially or ideologically.

72

Fourth, participation in international cooperation will symbolize their maturity and their pride in a newly acquired self-determination.

The enthusiastic participation of Southeast Asian countries in international affairs will undoubtedly take the form of alignment with the small nation bloc, which attempts whenever possible to determine questions on the principle of equity rather than power and in terms of economic self-reliance rather than world trade. The representatives of these nations to the United Nations with a few exceptions may not necessarily be either strong or sophisticated persons for some decades to come. The foreign relations of these countries for too many years have not been in their hands or even in their purview. The representatives will be asked to operate in a world dominated by European cultural goals and techniques for which they have inadequate preparation in education and often even in language. The old superiority pattern of the colonial countries will still affect to a greater or lesser degree interpersonal relationships in the international scene.

From the point of view of the south Asian countries I should be willing to prognosticate that participation in the affairs of the United Nations will be a disillusioning one. However, their need for international affiliations will be none the less great. The choice will be between allying themselves with power blocs as satellite voters or to form their own bloc, their own inward-turning affiliations. The probability of the latter course seems high.

In the field of international relations are the nations of Southeast Asia likely to draw together into a closer unit? Certainly in the last two hundred years the policy of European nations served to separate the areas they controlled.

But now suggestions for regional organizations are in the air. The idea of a federation of Southeast Asian countries is not new. During the war it was suggested in both the United States and Great Britain by private persons. This suggestion has taken various forms and had varying motives. Recently it has been suggested again in the United States in the form of a United Nations consultation commission. The United Kingdom and Australia have also recently initiated some action in this direction. These suggestions as a device for tempering colonial administration are now too late to be implemented by external powers unless there is internal support for the move.

Certainly, the interest among Southeast Asian leaders in each other and in a rapprochement between their countries is keen and appears to be growing. The earliest suggestion known to me came from Romulo of the Philippines in the form of a Pan-Malayan Union. Since then the idea appears to have occurred independently to other nationalists. At the moment, naturally, a federation of Southeast Asian nations is no more than a vague idea of a few men. There are, however, many forces that may encourage the growth of such union in one or another form. The weakness of each country by itself is apparent to all. The disillusionment of these first three years of peace does not promise to be abated for many years to come. There is furthermore a common interest in, and knowledge of, each other that did not exist before the war. During the colonial period the differences between the countries of Southeast Asia were accentuated by their different forms of administration and the differences between the metropolitan countries through which their knowledge of European culture filtered. Each colony was centered on its European administering country.

Until the war south Asians who may have spent many years abroad in study had seldom visited each other's countries or met their leaders. Today the picture has already altered. Aung San of Burma before his death, Ho Chih Minh of Indochina, Soekarno, and Sjahrir of Indonesia, Dato Omn bin Jafaar of Malaya, Romulo of the Philippines, and above all, Nehru of India, know and follow closely each other's actions. Increasingly in the future we may expect a turning inward of Southeast Asian people upon themselves. The leadership of India mentioned earlier is doing much to encourage and facilitate just this type of contact and to raise questions of common concern. Lastly, we must not forget that international affiliation and regional ties are very much part of the international political atmosphere into which the countries of Southeast Asia are now entering for the first time.

There are of course impediments. Although we have spoken consistently of Southeast Asia as a region, it is a series of only comparable, not identical, cultures. There are linguistic and religious differences. There is always the possibility that the Buddhist countries of Burma, Siam, and Indochina may find more in common among themselves than they would with the Malays of Malaya, Indonesia, and the Philippines. Although it is true that Siam has always had a certain uneasiness about her Burman neighbor, this may have been more toward the British in Burma than toward the Burmans themselves. Certainly, the Thai peoples from the Shan States of Burma through to Laos in Indochina form a single ethnic and linguistic bloc; and Thai Irredentism used to be a matter of some concern to certain British officials. Indochina and Indonesia are forging a common bond in their common revolutionary experience. Indonesia's affiliation with the

75

Philippines is also one of a common ethnic kinship. There will be real obstacles nevertheless. Malaysia's continued colonial status and the obvious continuation of Philippine dependence on the United States for assistance in its problems will not facilitate mutual confidence among the constituent nations of a Southeast Asian federation or bloc. Burma may be timid about India and its moneylenders who dominated the economy of the Irrawady Delta. If the Netherlands continue to dominate the foreign relations of Indonesia, if France can control those of the Vietnam, there will be real impediments to a free association of Southeast Asian countries.

Further impediments to rapprochement exist on the economic side. The countries of the area have all been developed in a parallel fashion. Each country was developed to meet the needs of an industrialized and mercantile European country. In periods of world depression, they are competing rather than complementary economies. Except to a very limited degree they are not a series of markets for each other's goods, nor are they able to supply themselves with industrial equipment. This economic situation does little to facilitate affiliations.

Whether or not some form of union becomes in the near future, a feasible and desirable solution for Southeast Asia, the nations of the world would presumably deplore seeing Southeast Asia becoming a new Balkans — a series of weak states which are the pawns of other powers. Nor must Chinese and Indian enclaves become the Sudeten lands of Asia. So long as the present socio-political trends indigenous to the area are allowed to express themselves, this seems an unlikely development. The possibilities, however, of the intrusion of external powers must not be ignored.